2004 POETRY C

ONCE UPON A RHYME

IMAGINATION FOR A NEW GENERATION

Herefordshire & Worcestershire

Edited by Sarah Marshall

Young**Writers**

First published in Great Britain in 2004 by:
Young Writers
Remus House
Coltsfoot Drive
Peterborough
PE2 9JX
Telephone: 01733 890066
Website: www.youngwriters.co.uk

SB ISBN 1 84460 637 6

Foreword

Young Writers was established in 1991 and has been passionately devoted to the promotion of reading and writing in children and young adults ever since. The quest continues today. Young Writers remains as committed to engendering the fostering of burgeoning poetic and literary talent as ever.

This year's Young Writers competition has proven as vibrant and dynamic as ever and we are delighted to present a showcase of the best poetry from across the UK. Each poem has been carefully selected from a wealth of *Once Upon A Rhyme* entries before ultimately being published in this, our twelfth primary school poetry series.

Once again, we have been supremely impressed by the overall high quality of the entries we have received. The imagination, energy and creativity which has gone into each young writer's entry made choosing the best poems a challenging and often difficult but ultimately hugely rewarding task - the general high standard of the work submitted amply vindicating this opportunity to bring their poetry to a larger appreciative audience.

We sincerely hope you are pleased with our final selection and that you will enjoy *Once Upon A Rhyme Herefordshire & Worcestershire* for many years to come.

Contents

Ashfield Park Primary School

Madeleine Maloney (11)   1
Bethany Hill (11)   2
Dalton Ruck (11)   3
Chloe White (10)   4
Nazira Tourmoche (11)   5
Sarah Lester (10)   6
Alexandra Arbourne (11)   7
Fiona Stephens (10)   8
Chloe Davies (11)   9
Glen Parry (11)   10
Madison Churchus (11)   11
Lawrence Minton (11)   12
Ben Gardner (11)   13
Martin Hogg (11)   14
Zoe Claire Burton (11)   15
Lauren Scott (11)   16
Charmaine Stevens (10)   17
Sarah Lewis (11)   18
Lisa Christopher (11)   19
Rachel Bedford (11)   20
Matthew Henshall (11)   21

Bromesberrow St Mary's CE Primary School

Carl Davies (11)   22
Cameron Lane (11)   23
William Sandercock (10)   24
Richard Watkins (11)   25
Chanel Lee (11)   26
Chayce Parslow (9)   27
Charlotte Hodges (10)   28
Luke Williams (9)   29
Hannah Trigg (9)   30
Edward Smith-Oakey (8)   31
Jarrod Jones (8)   32
Sam Hart (8)   33
Faye Harkins (9)   34
Matthew Hand (8)   35
David Feakins (9)   36

Danielle Blakeway (10)   37
Joe Boswell (10)   38

Cradley Primary School
Thomas Boldry (9)   39

Gorsley Goffs Primary School
Sean Morgan (11)   40
Jessica Drew (10)   41
Jake Howells (10)   42
Alex Goulding (9)   43
Moss Davis (11)   44
Rachel Hoskins (11)   45
Chris Marchant (10)   46
James Powell (11)   47
Ryan Clack (11)   48
Sarah Granby (10)   49
Ciara Ruth Hewitt (10)   50
Rysha Ketteridge-Flint (11)   51
Natalie Sidnell (9)   52
Jade South (11)   53
Ben James   54
Charlotte Milton (11)   55
Sam Hayes (11)   56
Katie Nixon (10)   57
Rybeka Parsons (11)   58
Charles Hiram (11)   59
Eleanor Blackwood (10)   60
Rebecca Gooch (11)   61
Mark Badham (10)   62
Camilla Dobson (11)   63

Holme Lacy Primary School
Matthew Lofthouse (10)   64
Otto Putland (10)   65
Denholm Smith (11)   66
Christopher Morris (11)   67
Amy Milsom Baker (9)   68
Lauren Hungerford (10)   69
Katie Ryan (11)   70
Liam Stroud (10)   71

Jasmine Morgan (11)   72
Ryan Kendrick (10)   73

Lindridge CE Primary School
Hamish Pulford (8)   74
Thea Bamber Hall (7)   75
Alice Williams (9)   76
Samuel Andrews (8)   77
Leanne Potter (8)   78
Charlotte Bradley (9)   79
Christina Redman (8)   80
Amy Mapp (9)   81
Eliza Thompson & Leanne Hargreaves (9)   82
Victoria Harris (9)   83
Samantha Matravers (9)   84
Ellie Mapp (8)   85
Callum Redding (8)   86
Joshua Thompson (11)   87
Jessica Powell (9)   88
Lottie Silver (10)   89

Longdon St Mary's CE Primary School
Joe Yeates (11)   90
Daisy Yeates (9)   91
Grace Woodward (11)   92
Sophie Whittaker (10)   93
Charlotte Webber (10)   94
Jude Wagstaff (10)   95
Rosanna Sinclair (10)   96
Jasmine Quiney (10)   97
Laura Scott (9)   98
Jack Larner (9)   99
Eleanor Kirby (10)   100
Alice Kerrigan (9)   101
Victoria Houghton (9)   102
Sophia Franklin (9)   103
Holly Barrett (9)   104

Oldbury Park Primary School
Bethany Austin (11)   105
Andy Baker (11)   106

Connor Murphy (10)   107
Natalie Page (10)   108
Ian Collins (11)   109
Becky Knight (11)   110
Lucy Beswick (11)   111
Kym Robbins (11)   112
Abbey Jenkins (10)   113
Stewart Roberts (10)   114
Stefanie Webb (11)   115
Lydia Davis (11)   116
Haidee Bradley (11)   117
Anthony Harrold (11)   118
Bethany Small (11)   119
Callum Stoneham (11)   120
Lisa James (11)   121
Chloe Guyatt (10)   122
Holly Hemming (11)   123
Jess Fassnidge (10)   124
Lois Noond (10)   125
Joshua Phillpotts (11)   126
Olivia Williams (11)   127
Jamie Jones (10)   128
Jessica Hobbs (11)   129
James Todd (11)   130
Mikel Real (11)   131
Becky Clark (10)   132
Amy Hodgetts (11)   133
Lauren Weston (11)   134
Robert Deamer (10)   135
Ryan Sneddon (11)   136
Christopher Holtom (11)   137
Alex Taylor (10)   138
Sam Bullock (10)   139
Jordan Edge (10)   140
Ryan Mapp (10)   141
Amy Tomlins (10)   142
Alice Molloy (11)   143
Sophie Gardner (11)   144
Lucy Gurney (10)   145

St Joseph's RC Primary School, Droitwich

Joseph Jameson (10)   146
Niamh Tipton (9)   147
James Crampton (10)   148
Thomas Weatherby (9)   149
Rebecca Pearson (10)   150
Samuel Garvey (10)   151
Joseph Comerford (10)   152

Suckley Primary School

Alec Burt (11)   153
Annie Shirt (10)   154
Thomas Sandry (11)   155
Wayne Scarratt (9)   156
Georgina Tabberer-Mills (10)   157
Philippa Jolliffe (10)   158
Thomas James (10)   159
Ben Paige (10)   160
James Perrett (8)   161
Dannielle Mifflin (9)   162
Joseph Scarratt (7)   163
Harry Fraser (8)   164
Jamie Bentley (8)   165
Judy Morris (8)   166

Wigmore Primary School

Teige Stewart (11)   167
Kayleigh Luscott (11)   168
Ben Tranter (11)   169
Richard Taylor (10)   170
Chloe Reid (10)   171
Samantha Manuel (10)   172
Abby Whiteman (10)   173
Sara Crooke (11)   174
Kelly Archer (9)   175
Harry Wright (9)   176

The Poems

The Feeling Of War

The moon's turning a fiery-red,
As people are shooting and falling down dead.

Bombs are screaming over me;
Sailing through the leaves of a nearby tree.

Making a frightful emotion,
I cover my ears, waiting for the explosion.

I'm lying in a muddy trench,
Trying to breathe through the awful stench.

Shells singing a terrible song;
As they go whizzing along.

Aeroplanes flying overhead,
All of us cowering here in dread.

I fight here day by day,
As the moon looks over from far away.

Madeleine Maloney (11)
Ashfield Park Primary School

A Wartime Dream

Underneath the shelter, dingy and dark,
Dreaming of a summer's day, the sun a bright spark.

In the green meadows with pretty flowers,
But then back to the war and its terrible powers.

The moans and screeches of air raid sirens,
Under my shelter made of iron.

Eating ice cream on a sandy beach,
That dream's too far away, it's hard to reach.

I love my dreams of flowers and the sun,
But that's not ever going to happen, till the war is done.

Bethany Hill (11)
Ashfield Park Primary School

War Blocks The Sun

The war has begun
And I can't see the sun.

I need my family,
Bed and security.

This is probably my worst nightmare,
The loud blasting bombs, falling everywhere.

I want to see through the darkness,
All I can see is the people's loneliness.

Dalton Ruck (11)
Ashfield Park Primary School

Star

I look at the stars and think of my dad
All this war is driving me mad.

I think of my dad, so shiny and bright
I need him now to hold me tight.

I picture his face in the moon
I hope that I can see him soon.

I need him now to say goodbye
So he can see me before I die.

Chloe White (10)
Ashfield Park Primary School

Moonlit War

I look up at the moon, so bright
And think about this dangerous fight.

I really do hate this war,
I honestly can't take anymore.

I look up at the moon and think of my wife,
I hope this war won't take my life.

I want to go home,
I'm all alone.

But then the moon drifts away
And I realise I have to stay.

Nazira Tourmoche (11)
Ashfield Park Primary School

War Calligram

As I sit, weak, blood trickles down my arm
I can hear the screeching of an alarm.

My mind blanks out, I can see a dove,
All I can think of now, is love.

I hear a scream of laughter
My children are playing, they get happier and happier.

I hear beautiful songs of birds tweeting
The gentle wind whistling.

The bullets don't stop, the war carries on
I will have to keep dreaming and staying strong.

Sarah Lester (10)
Ashfield Park Primary School

War

I am a soldier in the Second World War,
The fighting goes on, more and more.

As I lie in the silent night,
The wind blows with all its might.

As I dream, I see,
People looking over me.

The sun is shining really bright,
It is a wonderful sight.

I see the grass swaying in the breeze,
Then suddenly, I freeze.

I see my children and wife,
Living a wonderful life.

I start to cry,
As I look into my wife's eye.

I suddenly wake,
As I am taken . . . out to war.

Alexandra Arbourne (11)
Ashfield Park Primary School

A Calligram

Here I'm sitting, looking up at the sky,
Looking up at the sky with my sleepy eye.

There are cries of pain from everywhere,
I wish I could get out of this crucial nightmare.

So I imagine what it was like before,
Before this terrible, brutal war.

The birds would sing peacefully in the trees,
With no wind at all, except a calm, calm breeze.

I remember my children and my wife,
They'll always be the main part of my life.

I wish to be at home, eating bread and butter,
But I'm still buried in a heap of clutter.

Here I'm sitting, looking up at the sky,
Looking up at the sky with my sleepy eye.

Fiona Stephens (10)
Ashfield Park Primary School

Calligram War

As I lie awake, I see a dove
I miss the people who I love.

As the metal bullets fly over me, I see
My children playing as happy as could be.

The trench which I lie in soaking in mud
Reminds me of my dog digging in the mud
The water in the trench runs like a big flood.

As I see the bombs exploding in the sky
It is like the sun
As I fall asleep, I think of my chum.

Chloe Davies (11)
Ashfield Park Primary School

Kill The Cockroaches

You kill,
With skill,
They are sly,
When you pass by,
We are scaring,
They are daring,
They better hide,
Or I'll take them for a ride,
But it's fun,
When they run
Crunch!

Glen Parry (11)
Ashfield Park Primary School

The Spider On The Book

It's over there, on that book!
Moving so very quick,
If I squash it, will it stick?
It's so hairy,
It's so scary,
Quick come and take a look.

Chuck it in the bin!
It's going to be dead,
I shall whack it on the head,
It's so small,
But boy, can it crawl,
Too many legs on that thing.

Maybe if you look really hard,
It really isn't that bad,
It looks sort of sad,
No one loves him,
No one likes him,
No one cares at all.

Madison Churchus (11)
Ashfield Park Primary School

Spider

Spider, spider, is so hairy,
Always likes to be scary.
Please don't fall,
Off the wall,
You're so small,
You like to crawl.
If something goes in your web,
They will be dead.

Lawrence Minton (11)
Ashfield Park Primary School

The Spider

Spinning a web
Until it's dead,
Very hairy
When it's scary,
Very small
When it wants to crawl
When it comes to his doom
It likes to come into people's rooms.

Ben Gardner (11)
Ashfield Park Primary School

The Spider

In its home the spider scuttles,
In the tree, leaves it rustles,
Each leg,
Is like a peg,
Its toes are like a hook,
Little girls it does spook,
It decides to spy,
On a passing fly,
The spider then jumps,
The fly's one of the lumps,
In the spider's web,
Then it is dead,
The spider gives a chuckle of glee
And says, 'There's more dinner for me!'

Martin Hogg (11)
Ashfield Park Primary School

Spider

Spider, spider on the wall,
Please don't fall,
You're so hairy,
You're so scary,
You're so small
And love to crawl,
I like your web,
Even though flies are dead.

Zoe Claire Burton (11)
Ashfield Park Primary School

Snail

A gross thing is the snail,
it always leaves a slimy trail,
it likes dark, gloomy places
and leaves behind ugly traces,
you might find it in your shed,
eyes popping out of its head,
is it hiding in its shell?
I will never, never tell.

Lauren Scott (11)
Ashfield Park Primary School

The Spider

The spider who I saw, is very hairy
And is very cruel.
Spider, you're so rough,
Spider, you're really tough.
You scuttle along the floor so hard,
You also make the leaves rustle.
Spider, you're so small,
Spider, you're so cruel.

Charmaine Stevens (10)
Ashfield Park Primary School

The Wasp

The wasp has a sting,
So watch your wing,
The wasp eats flies,
So he must be a spy,
The wasp is rough
And is very, very tough,
The wasp is bright
And is definitely light,
The wasp is hairy
And is very scary.

Sarah Lewis (11)
Ashfield Park Primary School

The Spider

They're mean,
They're unclean,
They are small,
They crawl,
They creep,
They eat,
They're hairy,
They're *so* scary,
They're good climbers,
That's the spider!

Lisa Christopher (11)
Ashfield Park Primary School

My Snail Friend

There is a snail I know,
He goes very slow,
He wears a colourful shell
And goes by the name of Mel,
He is rather grimy
And very, very slimy,
He moves along the ground
And makes not a sound.

Rachel Bedford (11)
Ashfield Park Primary School

The Wasp

The wasp is rough,
The wasp is tough,
His body is just a ball of fuzz,
When he flies, you hear his buzz,
It comes from his wing,
Watch out for his sting.

Matthew Henshall (11)
Ashfield Park Primary School

Playjagog

I am a whizzing, wobbly, slimy fog,
A greenish colour and smell like a hog,
Brother of wind, cousin of fire,
If you mess with me,
The consequences will be dire,
I'm as big as a jet
And as small as a die,
I'm in your brain,
I'm eating your pie,
I'm not vain,
This is no lie.

Carl Davies (11)
Bromesberrow St Mary's CE Primary School

Good Vs Evil

I am Falketord, a great valley river,
I am Zargoraw, a horrible feeling
That will make you shiver.

I am Falketord, I will not bite,
I am Zargoraw, a selfish parasite.

I am Falketord, as bright as the sun,
I am Zargoraw, I am the evil one.

I am Falketord, I am not a dream, I am real,
I am Zargoraw, I am as hard as a rock
And have nerves like steel.

Cameron Lane (11)
Bromesberrow St Mary's CE Primary School

Tefree

I could be antifreeze,
I will be a bird going higher,
I will be the sun creeping closer,
I am a ball of fire,
I dream of being the global ice wind.

William Sandercock (10)
Bromesberrow St Mary's CE Primary School

The African Lion Hunter!

A chocolate chamber,
A brutal bully,
A hard harrier,
Sneaking across the dry savannah,
Her fly swat out of control as her feet start to roll,
Raging ridge on her back,
Getting ready to attack,
Ready to pounce she sees her prey,
But the rest of her gang has lost their way,
Courage takes over as she bounds,
Her feet metres off the ground,
A wild roar lets loose,
She pounces,
She strikes,
Blood . . .

Richard Watkins (11)
Bromesberrow St Mary's CE Primary School

Monsahon

My name is Monsahon, Monsahon,
No one knows what I look like,
Like a peapod just popped open,
Like an orange being squeezed,
Like an apple just been bitten into,
My name is Monsahon, Monsahon.

Chanel Lee (11)
Bromesberrow St Mary's CE Primary School

Flanboxagan

I am the sole within your yearning for power,
I will be the bitter Arctic wind that wakes in the north and in the west,
I am not the coward that runs about like a chicken,
I will be the knife that kills you.

Chayce Parslow (9)
Bromesberrow St Mary's CE Primary School

The Teacher

I am a teacher,
Rabballbeet,
I'm not an angry person,
Maths, English get it right,
Or you will have a fright,
I don't help stuck children,
'Get on with it!' I say,
Glad when I get home,
Away from children for tonight,
They will be up all night,
With the ton of homework they have got.

Charlotte Hodges (10)
Bromesberrow St Mary's CE Primary School

Zufootca

I am Zufootca
I am Zufootca
I'm as speedy as thunder
And I sound like wonder
I am Zufootca
I am Zufootca
I dream of being the oceans blue
I only wish it could be true.

Luke Williams (9)
Bromesberrow St Mary's CE Primary School

Darkazeb, Darkazeb

Darkazeb, Darkazeb
I'm as delicate as a spider's web
We will never go to bed
Darkazeb, Darkazeb
You can come along with me
I will take you to the sea
Darkazeb, Darkazeb
I will show you my auntie
She's big, fat and lazy
Darkazeb, Darkazeb.

Hannah Trigg (9)
Bromesberrow St Mary's CE Primary School

My Job Is Poetry

My job is poetry
My poetry is art
But hey, sometimes it's easy
Sometimes it's like Bart
Sometimes it's scary, scary as can be
And I don't want to start:

I want to just keep going
It does not stop
Until the day is over
And my brain goes pop!
Excellent, excellent, excellent
Poem.
I will do it
And I will show them
I will show them
How it's done
I will show them
How it's fun!

Edward Smith-Oakey (8)
Bromesberrow St Mary's CE Primary School

Cheewresaru

Cheewresaru, Cheewresaru, I am a bulb flashing on and off.
Sometimes I have a bit of a cough.
Cheewresaru, Cheewresaru, am I alive or am I dead?
I sleep in a pigsty instead.
Cheewresaru, Cheewresaru, it's time to go.
So see you next time on the show.

Jarrod Jones (8)
Bromesberrow St Mary's CE Primary School

Great White Shark - Haiku

Great white shark eats fish
Tummy as white as a cloud
Teeth as sharp as knives.

Sam Hart (8)
Bromesberrow St Mary's CE Primary School

Lion - Haiku

This creature is wild
It likes lots and lots of meat
Mostly it will eat.

Faye Harkins (9)
Bromesberrow St Mary's CE Primary School

The Newt - Haiku

Newts blow big bubbles
Newts drink lots of fresh water
Newts swim very fast.

Matthew Hand (8)
Bromesberrow St Mary's CE Primary School

Footsudo

I am a big bird swooping in circles
Footsudo, Footsudo
I hop further than a frog
Footsudo, Footsudo.

David Feakins (9)
Bromesberrow St Mary's CE Primary School

Dog - Haiku

Furry ears, tail wags
He's a sweet and cuddly thing
He lives in the house.

Danielle Blakeway (10)
Bromesberrow St Mary's CE Primary School

Cheafadeas

I am Cheafadeas
Maybe I could be a loaf of peas
I am good, I am bad
Nobody knows
I dodge through flames
I swerve through air
With my hard back tail
And my flamy breath
I can do anything
Yes, anything
Anything.

Joe Boswell (10)
Bromesberrow St Mary's CE Primary School

Cars

Cars go fast
Cars go slow
Cars go every speed
You want them to go
Cars come in all shapes and sizes
Cars come small
Cars come big
Cars.

Thomas Boldry (9)
Cradley Primary School

Happiness Feels . . .

Happiness is lime green, slithering down a stick.
Happiness is like eating a KFC meal in Burger King.
Happiness smells like a fifty pound note fresh from the factory.
Happiness sounds like a Nissan Skyline revving up its engine
                                        with nitro.
Happiness feels like world domination and full control.

Sean Morgan (11)
Gorsley Goffs Primary School

Love In My Thoughts

Love is red, red as a rose blown
In a cool summer's breeze.
It tastes of lavender from scented oil,
Heated by a warming candle.
Love is the smell of melting chocolate,
Drifting through the air.
It sounds like classical music,
With violins and harps strummed by delicate fingers.
Love looks like two bubbles coming closer,
Becoming one, love grows, but sometimes bursts.

Jessica Drew (10)
Gorsley Goffs Primary School

Anger

Anger is as black as a river filled with dead bodies,
It tastes of poison, killing people with one spoonful,
Anger is the smell of ashes, ashes from a burnt-out fire,
It sounds like the haka of New Zealand going to war,
Anger looks like water trying to force its way into the cliff,
With every last ounce of energy.

Jake Howells (10)
Gorsley Goffs Primary School

Anger

Anger is thick crimson blood trickling down your face.
It tastes of sharp peppers.
Like a bomb exploding inside your mouth.
Anger is the smell of onions, being finely chopped.
It sounds like blackboards getting scratched by long finger nails.
Anger looks like a storm, in the darkness.

Alex Goulding (9)
Gorsley Goffs Primary School

Fear

Fear is the deepest black, like the midnight sky.
It tastes of smoke wafting into my lungs, choking me.
Fear is the smell of ashes.
It sounds like the clanging of pans smashing together.
Fears looks like the darkness in the shadows.

Moss Davis (11)
Gorsley Goffs Primary School

Love Is Like . . .

Love is pink like the opening of a rose
growing in the meadow.
It sounds like singing birds, high in the tree
talking their own language.
Love looks like a freshly baked cake
waiting to be eaten.
It tastes like chocolate strawberries
fresh out of the box.
Love is the smell of scented candles
flickering around the room.

Rachel Hoskins (11)
Gorsley Goffs Primary School

Happiness

Happiness is the colour of a daffodil flapping in the zephyr.
It tastes of melted chocolate dripping from your mouth.
Happiness is the fragrant smell of a summer's afternoon,
The sun shining down.
It sounds like Lost Prophets booming in my bedroom.
It looks like a smiley face looking at me.

Chris Marchant (10)
Gorsley Goffs Primary School

Happiness

Happiness is the colour of a daffodil,
blowing through the cool breeze.
It tastes of a delicious roast chicken,
on a Sunday afternoon, sizzling on my tongue.
Happiness is the smell of a freshly grown strawberry
shining in the sun, under the small oak tree.
It sounds like a loud trumpet,
echoing through the countryside.
Happiness looks like the sun
gleaming through the trees on a summer's day.

James Powell (11)
Gorsley Goffs Primary School

Shy

Shy is the colour of turquoise, of a light green leaf.
It tastes like turkey sandwiches at my cousin's,
When I'm too shy to take one.
Shy smells like dead turkey that squealed at the sight of a knife.
It sounds like silence when I'm shy, until the turkey suffers.
Shy looks like sweet depression and tiredness.

Ryan Clack (11)
Gorsley Goffs Primary School

Happiness

Happiness is ochre, baby-blue, camomile,
        a smile with a wink
        on the side.
It tastes of beautiful cottage pie
        fresh out of the oven.
Happiness is the aroma of flowers
        in the wild and mixed
        into perfume.
It sounds like a giggle, a laugh,
        the chorus of a seashell.
Happiness looks like a just-born baby
        and lambs bleating in the
        meadows.

Sarah Granby (10)
Gorsley Goffs Primary School

My Way Of Happiness

Happiness is the colour of a meadow full of violets.
The taste of a double chocolate fudge cake just right for anyone.
Happiness is the fragrance of a field full of lavender in rows all so neat.
Happiness is the sound of silence when only the distant voices
can be heard with a whistle of the birds.
Happiness is a smile full of laughter and a warmth of joy.

Ciara Ruth Hewitt (10)
Gorsley Goffs Primary School

Anger

Anger is blood-red that sizzles and burns under your skin.
It tastes of hot spicy curry that shoots down your throat like electricity.
Anger is the smell of ashes and smoke from a burning fire swirling
into the cold, dark night.
It sounds like a volcano waiting to erupt to release red-hot
dispersing death.
Anger looks like a ferocious tiger, bright orange eyes seeking its prey.

Rysha Ketteridge-Flint (11)
Gorsley Goffs Primary School

Happiness Is . . .

Happiness is the colour of a full moon,
sailing across a pitch-black sky.
The taste of a cone of caramel ice cream,
on a summer's night feeling it melt on my tongue.
Happiness is the fragrance of six red roses,
in a gloomy corner in the middle of nowhere.
It sounds like a robin singing,
on a Christmas Day, standing on a perch.
Happiness looks like a newborn baby,
with a slight smile, while in its mother's arms.

Natalie Sidnell (9)
Gorsley Goffs Primary School

Happiness

Happiness is the colour of bluebells,
the colour in my room.
It tastes of roast chicken baking in the oven,
all the vegetables sitting on the table.
Happiness is the smell of sweets
hanging in the air of a sweet shop.
It sounds like little lambs on a spring day,
bouncing in the field.
Happiness looks like my pony jumping in the meadow,
his coat shining in the sun.

Jade South (11)
Gorsley Goffs Primary School

Love

Love is red, like a big, juicy cherry,
shining in a tree.
It tastes of dark chocolate
melting on your tongue.
Love is the aroma of chocolate cookies
baked in the oven.
It sounds like laughter in the distance
giggling away, children having fun.
Love looks like two floppy arms
giving you a great . . . big . . . hug.

Ben James
Gorsley Goffs Primary School

Shade Of Green

Envy is emerald-green, that lurks in shadows.
It tastes of fudge all chewy and sweet, all locked away.
Envy is the aroma of strawberry jelly taunting me.
I can't reach but they can.
It sounds like ivy rustling up the shed door.
Envy looks like someone criticising you.
You can see their toy is better than yours, you want one.

Charlotte Milton (11)
Gorsley Goffs Primary School

Happiness

Happiness is a bright sun, yellow and beautiful.
It tastes of chocolate sponge cake, smooth and soft.
Happiness is the smell of summer fruits, juicy and fresh.
It sounds like the purring of a happy cat,
                    curled up in front of a warm oven.
Happiness looks like a beautiful, warm sunset,
rising from the west.

Sam Hayes (11)
Gorsley Goffs Primary School

Sadness Senses

Sadness is blue, a deep, dark blue, sending silent messages.
It tastes of salt tears, trickling down wet cheeks.
It's the scent of dampness, as it creeps silently around.
The sound of a weeping child, neglected and left unloved.
Sadness looks like the night sky, a deep, dark blue.

Katie Nixon (10)
Gorsley Goffs Primary School

Anger Is Red!

Anger is red, blood-red, orange, bright as fruit,
yellow like the sun.
It looks like ferocious fires, spreading rapidly,
tearing trees out of their paths.
Anger smells of an extra strong onion,
that's just been chopped, making tears.
It tastes of bitter lemon juice, squeezed from rotten lemons,
left of the side, lime green.
Anger sounds like the thumping of a million drums,
warriors about to go to war.
It's red, blood-red, orange, bright as fruit,
Yellow like the sun.

Rybeka Parsons (11)
Gorsley Goffs Primary School

Frightening Fear!

Fear is a deep, bleak grey,
    leaking out of an unwanted paint pot.
It tastes of horrible, powdery ash,
    scurrying into a dark, hidden crevice.
Fear is the smell of unused diesel,
    left lying in a rusty oil can.
It sounds like a high-pitched shriek,
    wailing in the midnight storm.
Fear looks like a wary, tattered ghost,
    haunting a deserted castle.

Charles Hiram (11)
Gorsley Goffs Primary School

Anger

Anger is black with hate,
   helplessly searching for light, without hope.
It tastes of ashes burning in your mouth,
   with nothing to put it out.
Anger is the smell of poison,
   hunting for revenge.
It sounds like buzzing in your head,
   telling you it has arrived.
Anger looks like water smashing into a cliff,
   waiting for a kill.

Eleanor Blackwood (10)
Gorsley Goffs Primary School

It Makes Sense!

Happiness is the colour of miniature crocuses,
dotted all around the garden.
It tastes of melted chocolate,
tumbling off the edge of Niagra Falls.
Happiness is the fragrance of a vanilla plant,
growing on an exotic island far away.
It sounds like a thundering helicopter,
about to lift its passengers high into the air.
Happiness looks like a newborn puppy,
bounding around the cold floor
and playing with chew toys.

Rebecca Gooch (11)
Gorsley Goffs Primary School

Hate

Hate is ebony like a piece of coal,
shining in the dark.
It tastes of chicken madras,
burning the back of your throat, numbing your tastebuds.
Hate is the smell of fresh sewage, that won't go away,
lingering all around you.
It sounds like the eruption taking over.
Hate looks like stew, slowly simmering,
then suddenly boiling out of the pan.

Mark Badham (10)
Gorsley Goffs Primary School

Anger!

Anger is a deep blood-red,
it sizzles and boils through you like electricity, wired to your mind.
It tastes of bitter fear, burning jealousy and black-sour hate,
chewing at your insides, a feeling you can't ignore.
Anger is the choking aroma of burning wood, drowning in fire,
causing grey smoke to swirl into the cold, black night.
It sounds like the hissing and spitting of a black cat,
dark as the underworld, noises sharp as a knife cut into your mind.
Anger looks like red-hot Hell, fingers of flame, scarlet, orange
                                                    and gold,
leaping and spitting, dancing into your heart, filling it with the heat
                                                    of the fire.

Camilla Dobson (11)
Gorsley Goffs Primary School

The World Of Hawaii

Smell the flowers,
Hear the sea,
Taste the sea salt in the air,
See the seagulls calling out to sea,
It's a brilliant place to be.

The sea is lapping on the beach,
Sun up high in the sky,
Watch the beach balls fly and fly,
Tingling feeling inside you,
People picking ripe fruits off palm trees.

Children building sandcastles,
Beautiful sunsets,
Lava erupting from a volcano's crater,
Dolphins jumping up high,
Ice cream van on the beach.

People surfing on the sea,
Multicoloured fish underwater,
Perfect place for holidays,
Girls doing hula,
This is the world of Hawaii!

Matthew Lofthouse (10)
Holme Lacy Primary School

Reggie, Who Never Shuts Gates

There was a man called Reggie Yates,
Who never thought of shutting gates.
It happened in the middle of May
That Reggie went on holiday.

Reggie forgot to shut his gates
And left on show his china plates.
While he was having fun in Spain,
Well away from all the rain.

Some people passing Reggie's home
Saw that it was all alone.
They went inside and looked around
Then took the plates, without a sound.

Once they had taken Reggie's plates,
They went outside and told their mates.
Within an hour most things were gone,
And all that was left, was a light that shone.

The very next day Reggie returned,
A valuable lesson he had learned.
A silly man called Reggie Yates
Learned always, always to shut gates.

Otto Putland (10)
Holme Lacy Primary School

One School Day

On the trip to school one day,
I saw a teacher on my way.
As I got up to the school gates,
I saw my mum talking to Mr Bates.
As I got to my first lesson,
Mr Bates burst into the room and shouted,
'James Crain,' to Mrs Hesson.
As I walked down the corridor wondering what I'd done this time.
I thought Mr Bates thought I had committed a terrible crime.
Lunchtime came soon after,
Filling the whole lunch hall with laughter.
When I'd finished my lunch, I went to my next lesson
And 'Oh no!' the teacher is Mrs Hesson.
When she gave me the homework from last week,
It made me look like a total geek.
Quickly I gave it her back
And she stuck it on the board with Blu-tack.
Everybody took the mick
And I gave my mate Billy, an almighty kick.
So there you are, that's one typical school day.

Denholm Smith (11)
Holme Lacy Primary School

Have You Ever Been Face To Face
With A Great White?

Have you ever been face to face with a great white?
If you have, it would give you a terrible fright.
Have you ever been face to face with a blue whale?
If you have, you would be flipped out of the water with its tail.
Have you ever been face to face with a fish?
I have! It was in my dish.

Have you ever been face to face with a snake?
If you're not careful you would make a mistake.
Have you ever been face to face with a black bear?
If you have, it would give you a terrifying scare.
Have you ever been face to face with a parrot?
I have! It was eating a carrot.

Have you ever been face to face with a ferret?
If you take it into school, you will get a merit.
Have you ever been face to face with a cat?
If you have, it would chase after a rat.
Have you ever been face to face with a dog?
I have! It gave me a big snog.

Christopher Morris (11)
Holme Lacy Primary School

The Butterfly

The little butterfly flies so high
Down to the ground, then to the sky
As she flutters she sees a bee
Making honey for his tea.
She sends sparkle dust wherever she flies
Always in the same, pretty guise
Where does she live? Perhaps in a bush
Is she very graceful? Does she ever push?
She soars up to a little white cloud
Only to find she's never loud
She flits shimmering from flower to flower
Releasing her own magical power.
Over the roses collecting nectar
Meeting her friend, caterpillar Hector
Nobody can ever hear her sing
Away she flaps with a *ping, ping, ping!*

Amy Milsom Baker (9)
Holme Lacy Primary School

The White Tiger

The white tiger crawls,
Waiting for its prey,
It will pounce, then creep away,
The white tiger has hidden powers,
It prowls through streams and pretty flowers,
The white tiger rests among the trees,
In shade beneath the colourful leaves,
Beautiful views across the land,
Looking at the country, isn't it grand,
But the white tiger wants more,
So off it goes with a *roar, roar, roar!*

Lauren Hungerford (10)
Holme Lacy Primary School

The Sun

When you go in the sun,
It is such fun,

You can have a water fight
And there is lots of light,

You can go on the beach,
Swim in the sea,

It is fun,
In the sun!

Katie Ryan (11)
Holme Lacy Primary School

Planes, Trains And Automobiles

Watch a plane flying by,
Faster than a blinking eye,
If you've seen a plane before,
It would let a mighty roar.

Beautiful countries it will see,
Smiling people looking at me,
America, Canada, Spain, the lot,
The plane's as big as a little spot,
Every day it's the same,
Anyone who thinks it's tame.

They're sadly mistaken.

Liam Stroud (10)
Holme Lacy Primary School

The Sun

Burning brightly in your eye
Is the sun bigger than the sky?
It blisters your skin
But don't be scared of the sun.

Jasmine Morgan (11)
Holme Lacy Primary School

Tractors

I can see mud in the air
And tractors going faster than you
Can you hear engines? I can!
Can you smell smoke?
I can see the trailer wobbling
Do you?
Can you hear starting pistols going off?
See how big the tyres are!

Ryan Kendrick (10)
Holme Lacy Primary School

There Was A Young Lady

There was a young lady from France
Who always had smelly pants
One day she wet the bed
'Oh dear!' is what she said
Oh, that poor young lady from France.

Hamish Pulford (8)
Lindridge CE Primary School

The Lady Called Loon

There once was a lady called Loon
Who jumped and jumped up to the moon
She saw a big rocket
And looked at her locket
And she jumped back down from the moon.

Thea Bamber Hall (7)
Lindridge CE Primary School

There Once Was A Man Of Ibeen

There once was a man of Ibeen
Who decided to eat ice cream
He got in a pickle
His ice cream did trickle
That pickly man of Ibeen.

Alice Williams (9)
Lindridge CE Primary School

I Have A Big Brother Called Jules

I have a big brother called Jules
Who will never obey the rules
He got locked in the shed
Till it was time for bed
But he escaped using Dad's tools.

Samuel Andrews (8)
Lindridge CE Primary School

There Was A Young Lady Called Eve

There was a young lady called Eve
Who wore coats with very long sleeves
In the long month of May
She would sit every day
And sneeze and sneeze into her sleeves.

Leanne Potter (8)
Lindridge CE Primary School

There Once Was An Old Man Called Bill

There once was an old man called Bill
And he liked to play in the mill
The only thing he said
Was 'I have to be fed bread'
That silly old man called Bill.

Charlotte Bradley (9)
Lindridge CE Primary School

The Monkey Who Was Funky

There once lived a little donkey
Who wanted a furry monkey
Together they ate cake
That they both liked to bake
They thought they were very funky!

Christina Redman   (8)
Lindridge CE Primary School

The Young Lady Of France

There was a young lady of France
Who just loved to dance and to dance
One day she fell over
In a bed of clover
The silly young lady of France.

Amy Mapp (9)
Lindridge CE Primary School

The Punk Of Dundee!

There was a young punk of Dundee
Whose hair was stripy like a bee
He married a nice girl
Who owned a great big pearl
They lived forever happily.

Eliza Thompson & Leanne Hargreaves (9)
Lindridge CE Primary School

There Was A Young Woman From France

There was a young woman from France
Who always wore bright frilly pants
When on holiday in Spain
She fell over a drain
And gave all the Spaniards a glance.

Victoria Harris (9)
Lindridge CE Primary School

Bill

There once was an old man called Bill
Who swallowed a poisonous pill
But they thought he was dead
So they put him to bed
His mum had a look at his will.

Samantha Matravers (9)
Lindridge CE Primary School

There Was A Young Girl Called Toni

There was a young girl called Toni
Who had a little brown pony
He always ate his hay
He ate it every day
The girl with the lovely brown pony.

Ellie Mapp (8)
Lindridge CE Primary School

Football

The ball
He kicks it far
He scores
The crowd goes wild
The ref drops the ball
He kicks it
They win.

Callum Redding (8)
Lindridge CE Primary School

Death

The murderer grips his rusty knife,
To kill his one desire,
His heart as black as coal,
His eyes as if on fire.

He steps up to the window
And breaks out all the glass,
It stabs him in the arm,
His fist a bloody mass.

The owner of the house,
Doesn't see him there,
Before the morn has come,
The owner's been skinned bare!

Joshua Thompson (11)
Lindridge CE Primary School

My Cat

My cat is called Marmy
She likes to sleep on my brother's bed,
She sits there very calmly,
But she needs to be fed,
Marmy doesn't like much to be happening,
And she hates it when there is a big *bang,*
She is very good at running,
Especially when she hears a big *clang*,
I love my cat Marmy!

Jessica Powell (9)
Lindridge CE Primary School

Daffodils

Daffodils standing, showing off their brightly coloured flowers,
Oozing out the most wondrous smell.
Standing silent by the riverside, deep in the tall grass.
Hidden from the bees that capture pollen
                             from their butter-yellow petals.
Cramped in-between other special flowers that are lodged
                             in those calm and quiet places.
Daffodils.

Lottie Silver (10)
Lindridge CE Primary School

Food Across The World

Boats, planes and trains
Bring all our food
That we take for granted
But it's what others planted.

Fruit, vegetables and meat
Are what we like to eat.

We all like to drink
And across the globe, all are linked
Boats, planes and trains
Bring all our food.

Joe Yeates (11)
Longdon St Mary's CE Primary School

Food

It's supermarket time on Saturday
Today I get a big, big trolley.
As I push it down the aisle
I see lots of bananas from Jamaica
Lots of oranges from Spain.
As we turn the big corner
There's a mountain of pizza from Italy
As we turn the next big corner
There're piles of noodles and rice
From China and Japan.
I fill my trolley high with food
From around the world.
It reaches the sky.

Daisy Yeates (9)
Longdon St Mary's CE Primary School

Foods From Different Countries

Britain has a lot of food,
Some from other countries,
Pizza from Italy,
Melons are from Mexico,
An exotic place with exotic fruits.
From China come noodles and rice,
From Japan we have sushi.

Different countries have different foods
So Britain can enjoy a mixture of everything.

Grace Woodward (11)
Longdon St Mary's CE Primary School

Different Foods

In England we are grateful
For what we have to eat.

Think yourselves lucky
That you've got something to munch for lunch.

These are some foods we are grateful for:

Melons, spaghetti, apples, noodles,
Pears, tomatoes, grapes, pasta,
Lemons, peas, bananas, potatoes,
Oranges, sweetcorn.

Although we can't grow all of these foods
We rely on people from different countries
To grow them for us
So we can enjoy a delicious meal.

Sophie Whittaker (10)
Longdon St Mary's CE Primary School

People Are Not That Different

People are not that different,
I know they have different ways to live,
Dress and eat.

I go home in the car,
I see different people, black people,
White people, yellow and brown.
Big people, little people, fat and thin.
People are not that different, I know.

People have different personalities,
Some people are funny, some are nice,
Others are shy,
People are not that different, I know.

People have different names,
Some are long, some are short.
People have names that are really
Unusual and hard to say,
People are not that different, I know.

Charlotte Webber (10)
Longdon St Mary's CE Primary School

Unique

Brown, white,
Black as the night,
People are all unique,
Different gods, different clothes,
Different food that we can eat
Different houses, different names
And lots and lots of different games
Muddy lanes, tarmac roads
Where loads of transport goes
Brown, white,
Black as the night,
People are all unique.

Jude Wagstaff (10)
Longdon St Mary's CE Primary School

Food, Clothes And Colours

Mexican, Indian, Italian too,
All of these people live in Britain
Their food is good and makes me happy.
There are curries and poppadoms that tempt me to eat.
There are pizzas and pasta that makes me faster.
There are pitta wraps and melon perhaps.

I like their clothes, all of the colours of the rainbow,
There are red and orange Indian saris
There are blue and black Mexican hats
There are white and red Italian dresses
All of the colours of the rainbow.

Rosanna Sinclair (10)
Longdon St Mary's CE Primary School

You And Me

You and me, are like a tree
The branches linked together
We will all be linked forever.

Black and white
It's not the sight
That matters to you and me
Religion, food, clothes and tradition
Everyone's the same to me.

Jasmine Quiney (10)
Longdon St Mary's CE Primary School

Not Like England

In Greece they have a siesta,
Not like England.
In Italy they make *giant* pizzas,
Not like England.
In Spain they eat paella,
Not quite like England.
In Wales they have lots of rain,
Very like England!

Laura Scott (9)
Longdon St Mary's CE Primary School

Multi-Cultural Food

Out around the world,
We eat different food,
Some Italian and some Chinese
And we all live in a multi-cultural world.

Jack Larner (9)
Longdon St Mary's CE Primary School

India

India is scorching hot
Not like England
They wear saris
And bright coloured tops, not like me or you
Back in England it's really cold and wet
They're laughing at us in India
Because we're so wet
But all of us are joined together
Whether we're black or white
Even if you're identical twins
Or really tall in height
We care and love one another
Like we're sisters and brothers
So care for our wonderful world
Because it's as precious as a glistening pearl.

Eleanor Kirby (10)
Longdon St Mary's CE Primary School

Walking Down The Street

Walking down the street,
These are the clothes that I will meet,
Indian women wear saris
And the English wear jeans, shorts and caps,
The Scottish wear kilts
And the Muslims wear bhurkas
And last but not least, Sikhs wear turbans.

Walking down the street,
These are the foods that I will meet,
Italian restaurants with pizza and pasta
And Chinese restaurants with noodles and rice,
The English restaurants with roast dinners
And Yorkshire puddings
And Indian restaurants with curries and poppadoms.

Walking down the street,
These are the people that I will meet,
Some are black and some are white,
All of us are different.

Alice Kerrigan (9)
Longdon St Mary's CE Primary School

Different Faces

People are black, white and brown.
We all live in different towns.
Different houses, clothes and blouses.
All of us are different.
All of us have different names.
None of us are really the same
Because that is how God made us.

Victoria Houghton (9)
Longdon St Mary's CE Primary School

Different People

Different language, different colour,
We are not different people altogether.
We all have two legs, two arms and one head.
It's just the way we were born.

Hindu, Christian, Muslim and Sikh,
Some speak Latin, French or Greek.
In the end we are all people,
People are just plain people.

Sophia Franklin (9)
Longdon St Mary's CE Primary School

All Of Us Are Different

All of us are different
Black or white
You can decide.

All of us are different
Some speak Dutch
Which I like so much.

All of us are different
Some support Hallowe'en
Which makes me scream.

All of us are different
Some are Sikh
With interesting food that they eat.

All the world is different
Some of us are black
Some of us are white
But all of us are different.

Holly Barrett (9)
Longdon St Mary's CE Primary School

Water

Storm starter,
Window banger,
Fear maker,
Fire fighter,
Body cleaner,
Flood maker,
Body needer,
House wrecker,
Heart breaker.

Bethany Austin (11)
Oldbury Park Primary School

Fire Kennings

Life taker,
Flame flicker,
Family threatener,
Habitat destroyer,
Ash bringer,
Skin singe-er,
Flame leaper,
Earth wrecker,
Sound crackler,
Smoke bringer.

Andy Baker   (11)
Oldbury Park Primary School

Monkey

I am . . .
Swinger of the trees
Climber of the bushes
King of the jungle
Maker of branches
Eater of bananas
I kill no human.

I know . . .
The squealing of birds through the trees
And the sound of the biggest animal known to man
The swinging song
I kill no human.

Connor Murphy (10)
Oldbury Park Primary School

Water Kennings

Life helper
Drink giver
Fire fighter
Dirt cleaner
Plant helper
Heat killer
Thirst stopper
Food grower
Flood maker
Storm maker.

Natalie Page (10)
Oldbury Park Primary School

Lion

I am
The jungle king
Guardian of the lands
I protect my pride
I harm no man.

I know
Only the sounds of the forest
The sighs of the trees being blown
The legacy will never end
I harm no man.

Ian Collins (11)
Oldbury Park Primary School

Air Kennings

Whistle blower
Wave maker
Grass shaver
Wind blower
Wind maker
Cheek chiller
Body cooler
Life bringer
Tree waver
Air twister
Breath taker.

Becky Knight (11)
Oldbury Park Primary School

Air Kennings

Breeze maker
Seed shaker
Breath taker
Tree swayer
Cloud mover
Ice maker
Kite flyer
Heat breaker
Petal taker
Ripple maker.

Lucy Beswick (11)
Oldbury Park Primary School

Water Kennings

Life bringer
Fire fighter
Rain pourer
Grass soaker
Plant wetter
Sweat maker
Thirst killer
Wave constructor
Ice maker
Body freshener.

Kym Robbins (11)
Oldbury Park Primary School

Air

Tree shaker
Life saver
Body cooler
Breeze bringer
Frost maker
Cold bringer
Heat killer
Breath bringer
Bone shaker
Leaf raiser
Ice maker.

Abbey Jenkins (10)
Oldbury Park Primary School

Tree Frog

I am . . .
A woodland liver
Tree leaper
Maker of leaves
I eat no tadpoles.

I know . . .
Only the soft air of the forest
The branches and leaves of the forest
                        tapping on the trunks
The happy frog song at dusk and dawn
I eat no tadpoles.

Stewart Roberts (10)
Oldbury Park Primary School

Fire Kennings

Flame thrower
Heat blazer
Life taker
Family breaker
Fear maker
Death bringer
Skin burner
Home destroyer
Heart pounder
Scream sounder.

Stefanie Webb (11)
Oldbury Park Primary School

Air Kennings

Seed blower
Plant shaker
Tree waver
Tornado maker
Land destroyer
Illness bringer
Sheet dryer
Breath taker
Face chiller
Rain bringer.

Lydia Davis (11)
Oldbury Park Primary School

Cats And Kittens

We are,
Mouse hunters,
Land lovers,
Makers of territories,
We hunt all mice.

We know,
Only our collar bell sounds,
We pounce on our prey,
The sad cat and kitten song,
We love hunting mice.

Haidee Bradley (11)
Oldbury Park Primary School

Bird

I am . . .
King of flying
Glide ruler
Song maker
I eat all worms.

I know . . .
Only the leaves' tune in rough weather
The air from back to front at noon and night
The crying birds' song
I eat all worms.

Anthony Harrold (11)
Oldbury Park Primary School

Squirrel

I am . . .
Log sprinter
Tree nestler
Planter of seeds.
I destroy no man's home.

I know . . .
Only the clunk of falling acorns
The swish of my own tail
The anxious calls of a parent squirrel
All day and all night.
I destroy no man's home.

Bethany Small (11)
Oldbury Park Primary School

Cheetah

I am . . .
Yellow lightning,
Grass sprinter,
Maker of dust clouds.
I leave few men.

I know . . .
Only the barren wastelands of bone,
The hunt and life and death of my prey,
Few escape my wrath.
I leave few men.

Callum Stoneham (11)
Oldbury Park Primary School

Dolphin

I am . . .
Sea voyager,
Food maker,
Master of waves,
I harm all fish.

I know . . .
Only the fast tune of flying birds,
The flash of blood as the seas flow by,
The shining sun,
The happy dolphin song,
I harm all fish.

Lisa James (11)
Oldbury Park Primary School

Dolphin

I am . . .
Ocean traveller,
Wave pouncer,
Maker of echoes.
I help all men.

I know . . .
Only all the fish of the sea,
The crash and splash of the tide
Meeting land in the day and night,
The sweet dolphin sound.
I help all men.

Chloe Guyatt (10)
Oldbury Park Primary School

Polar Bear

Fur as white as snow,
As slick and cold as the ice.

Paws pounding in the cold snow,
Icebergs swimming on the gleaming water.

Kindly caring for its baby young,
There's polar bears pouncing and pounding
Everywhere they go.

Polar bears that are swimming along,
The gleaming water,
Watching their own reflection in the water.

Holly Hemming (11)
Oldbury Park Primary School

Budgie

I am . . .
Sky skimmer
Sky scraper
Tree sitter
Song singer
In danger I am.

I know . . .
Blazing heat
Air and freedom
Every branch on every tree
In danger I am.

Jess Fassnidge (10)
Oldbury Park Primary School

Fire Kennings

Face warmer
Spirits bringer
Oxygen destroyer
Flame dancer
Ground heater
Secret keeper
Flame burner
Smoke signer
Leaf burner.

Lois Noond (10)
Oldbury Park Primary School

The Polar Bear Song

Fur as warm as the morning sun,
Destroyed by the red of their blood.
Icebergs as high as towering skyscrapers,
To shelter them from danger.

Joshua Phillpotts (11)
Oldbury Park Primary School

I Am/I Know

I am . . .
As brave as a knight in armour,
Proud prowler,
King of the jungle,
Pride of the pack,
Master of disguise when hunting,
A killer, that's me.

I know . . .
Only the scorched earth around me,
The shade will cool me,
A killer, that's me.

Olivia Williams (11)
Oldbury Park Primary School

Snake

I am . . .
Hissing, slithering
Quiet creeper
Cold blooded
The silent seeker.

I know . . .
Only the heat of the sun
That keeps me warm,
Creeping about to trap my prey
In waving grass,
The silent seeker.

Jamie Jones (10)
Oldbury Park Primary School

Dolphin Song

I am . . .
Angel of the sea
Deep-sea diver
Ocean calmer
I want it to stay that way.

I know . . .
The song of the whale
The sonar of my friends
The colour of the fish
I want it to stay that way.

Jessica Hobbs (11)
Oldbury Park Primary School

Animal Song

I am . . .
Secret spyer,
Overlooker,
Giver of the unknown,
I never go low.

I know . . .
Only the fast movement of the stampede,
The power and strength of the safari crew awakening at sunrise,
The giraffe understanding,
I never go low.

James Todd (11)
Oldbury Park Primary School

Water Kennings

People slapper
Life renewer
Plant maker
Sea waker
Wave breaker
Earth swallower
Flame killer
Ocean keeper
Life taker
Fish supplier.

Mikel Real (11)
Oldbury Park Primary School

Turtle

I am . . .
> Gleam weaver
> Sleep dreamer
> The master of my environment.

I fear no one except for man.

I know . . .
> I may look clumsy on land
> In the water I can protect myself

My shell is my home
My beak can rip through flesh
My claws are like daggers
They tear through the bone.

Becky Clark (10)
Oldbury Park Primary School

Air Kennings

Silent breather
Ground shaker
Tree blower
Oxygen deliverer
People refresher
Earth rouser
Leaf faller
Bush breezer
Life saver
Fire feeder.

Amy Hodgetts (11)
Oldbury Park Primary School

I Am/I Know

I am . . .
Proud prowler
Food chaser
Protective father
I hunt intruders
King of the beasts.

I know . . .
The jungle fever
The whispering savannah
The animals there
The sound of creatures
My intruders know that I'm
King of the beasts.

Lauren Weston (11)
Oldbury Park Primary School

Fire Haiku

A flickering flame
Dancing in the midnight sky
Making people run.

Robert Deamer (10)
Oldbury Park Primary School

Water Kennings

Heat cooler
Sand sweeper
Bank licker
Bed sleeper
Stress healer
Cloud maker
Wave surfer
Surface skipper
Earth wetter.

Ryan Sneddon (11)
Oldbury Park Primary School

Fire Kennings

Heat giver
Wood burner
Flame thrower
Light giver
Dark smoker
Burning fear
Life taker
Flame dancer
Ice melter
Candle burner.

Christopher Holtom (11)
Oldbury Park Primary School

Polar Kennings

A great white silhouette endlessly
Stalking, hunger-driven,
Its coat glistening with waterproof hairs,
Lumbering through vast glacial valleys,
In a land where the sun never sets.

Alex Taylor (10)
Oldbury Park Primary School

I Am/I Know

I am . . .
Cloud sweeper
King of the sky
Sleeping harmlessly
In the old burrow tree
Down by the riverside
I lie without a sound
Delicately balanced
As I sweep the dust
Away from the lake.
    I harm no man.

I know . . .
Where the footing is firm
And water is low
Seeing gentle curves
Of meandering stream
Arching branches
Within the breeze.
    I harm no man.

Sam Bullock (10)
Oldbury Park Primary School

SATs Test - Haiku

Nerves start kicking in
Forty five minutes of hell
The test is finished.

Jordan Edge (10)
Oldbury Park Primary School

Water Kennings

Earth swallower
Breath taker
Bubble maker
Boat floater
People pusher
Life snatcher
Raindrop faller
Heat cooler
Dry wetter
Ship painter.

Ryan Mapp (10)
Oldbury Park Primary School

Owl

I am . . .
The master of the oak tree
Catching my prey on land
Swooping and swishing in the night
The light turns to dark
The wings of the masters
I harm no man.

I know . . .
The only highest places ever
Only in the sky
The mouse catcher ever to be told
My food of prey
Speed of light no one can see
I harm no man.

Amy Tomlins (10)
Oldbury Park Primary School

Tiger

I am . . .
Pride owner
Territory fighter
Maker of terror
I hunt all living things.

I know . . .
Only the scream of a man
The depths of the jungle deep and dark
The tiger's call
I hunt all living things.

Alice Molloy (11)
Oldbury Park Primary School

Dolphin

I am . . .
Ocean passenger
Sea guarder
Maker of waves
I hurt no man.

I know . . .
Only the slow swirling of the tide
The crashing water meeting the land
The sad dolphin song
I hurt no man.

Sophie Gardner (11)
Oldbury Park Primary School

Snake

I am . . .
Grass slitherer
Hiss master
Maker of mazes
I harm no man.

I know . . .
Only the slimy sound of slithering snakes
The hiss and movement of long, winding curves
At dusk until dawn
The scaly snake song
I harm no man.

Lucy Gurney (10)
Oldbury Park Primary School

A Recipe For Under The Sea

Ingredients:
600,000,000 litres of water
6oz of deadly, vigorous great white sharks
5 round stuffed pufferfish
2 leaves of spicy coral

1. Get the 600,000,000 litres of water, then add 5,000 pinches of salty
salt to it and stir thoroughly.
2. Weigh 6oz of deadly, vigorous sharks and gently place them into
the water.
3. Crack 5 pufferfish and stuff them with chilly air.
4. Get 2 spicy pieces of coral and add them to the salty water.
5. Once you have added all of the ingredients to the bowl, whisk
thoroughly for 10 minutes. Then stir slowly but well for 5 minutes.
6. Pour the living water from the bowl onto a smooth, flat surface.
Then pour it onto unused parts of the tropical, exotic Earth.

Joseph Jameson (10)
St Joseph's RC Primary School, Droitwich

A Recipe For An Under The Sea World

What you need:
200 waves
4,020,000oz coral
4,200,000 turtles
41,300,000oz sand

Take 4,200,000 of turtles and mix in a bowl roughly
with 400 teaspoons of seaweed.
Then beat in 200 waves.
Add 4,020,000oz of coral and cook in a super-large, hot ocean
for 40 minutes.
Lastly, take out of ocean and sprinkle on a lot of salty sand.
Leave to cool down and then let the fish jump and swirl
into the galloping ocean.

Niamh Tipton (9)
St Joseph's RC Primary School, Droitwich

A Recipe For Under The Sea

Ingredients:
2 handfuls of fine salt
4 cups of swirling water
20 million giant squid
5 funny clownfish
5 bits of floating coral
2oz of playful children
3 huge humpback whales
1 teaspoon of barracuda
1 silver moon

The recipe:
Take your handful of fine salt and pour all of it in the 4 cups of swirling water. Stir with a whisk and do this madly. Do this until you have done it for about 5 minutes and then stop. After that, drop in 20 million giant squids, 5 funny clownfish, 5 bits of wavy coral, 3 huge humpback whales, 2oz of playful children and one teaspoonful of barracuda. Then stir madly for 10 minutes. After that get the moon, hover it over the saucepan and push it to and fro. Watch the water and if it goes in the same direction as the moon, leave it to cool down. When it has cooled down, pour it into a bowl.

James Crampton (10)
St Joseph's RC Primary School, Droitwich

A Recipe For An Aquatic World

Ingredients:
1 lunar-related tide
A pinch of salt
10,000,000 litres of fresh water
500,000,000 kg of awe-inspiring aquatic life

1. Take 10,000,000 litres of fresh water and pour it onto an
                                        unoccupied planet.
2. Add a pinch of salt and stir vigorously until foaming.
3. Blow the lunar-related tide around the unoccupied planet until any
                            form of natural satellite materialises.
4. Place in the awe-inspiring aquatic life, whisk gently until signs of
                                        life appear.

Thomas Weatherby (9)
St Joseph's RC Primary School, Droitwich

A Recipe For Under The Sea

Ingredients:

50,000 litres of water
500oz sand
50oz coral
25 rocks (of all sizes)
100oz salt
30 dolphins
20 crabs
5 waves
18oz krill
32 whales (of all kinds)
6 octopuses

700 rainbow-coloured fish
6 sting rays
4 barracudas
15oz of pretty features
80 dancingfish
50 flying fish
900oz seaweed
10,000 different kinds of fish
5 lobsters
3 basking sharks
1 giant squid

First take the 50,000 litres of water and mix the salt in slowly. Then add the 500oz of sand and after that place the seaweed into the water. Drop the 25 rocks onto the sand. When you've done that, put the coral onto the rocks. Gently put the dolphins into the water, then add 10 crabs, put the 32 whales in the water, followed by 18oz of krill. Then add 500 rainbow-coloured fish and 50 flying fish. Add 4 barracudas and 6 stingrays. The 5 lobsters go in with 10 crabs and the 3 basking sharks. Get the 6 octopuses and the giant squid and place them in the water. Next add 5 waves. Lastly, put into the oven for one hour. When time is up, leave to cool and you have an under the sea world!

Rebecca Pearson (10)
St Joseph's RC Primary School, Droitwich

A Recipe For Under The Sea!

To make an under sea world you must:
Take 2 sand sharks
10 big rocks
25oz sand
6 blue whales
100 different coloured coral seeds
3 clown fish
9 hammerhead sharks
8 crabs
5 lobsters
900 waves
9 trillion litres of water
900oz salt
10 trillion acres of dug-up land

Put all the water in the dug-up land, then add the salt and mix. Throw in the coloured coral seeds, then spread the sand in the water. Release the clown fish into the water, then release all the other animals into the water. Finally, add the waves and voila! Your under sea world is made!

Samuel Garvey (10)
St Joseph's RC Primary School, Droitwich

A Recipe For Under The Sea

Ingredients:
5000oz salt
100,000,000 litres of water
20oz coral and seaweed
100,000,000oz sand
60 rocks
600 different types of fish, including barracudas and whales
3 octopuses
2 giant squid
2 whirlpools
60 waves

1. First put 5000oz of salt into the 100,000,000 litres of water.
2. Add 60 waves and check which way the wind is blowing.
3. Drop rocks in water and make sure the waves don't blow them away.
4. Take whirlpools and put them in the centre of the sea.
5. To make the bottom of the sea, place 100,000,000 acres of sand at the bottom.
6. Take 20oz of coral and let it grow in the rocky sands.
7. Scatter seaweed everywhere.
8. Take the 600 animals and spread them out all over the sea.
There you have it, your own sea.

Joseph Comerford (10)
St Joseph's RC Primary School, Droitwich

A Pirate's Life Kennings

Ship stealer
Ship sailor
Parrot shoulder
Parrot holder
Coffee trader
Coffee drinker
Gold snatcher
Gold bearer
Pistol loader
Pistol firer
Kidnapper
Kid killer
Royal catcher
Royal hanger.

Alec Burt (11)
Suckley Primary School

River Kennings

Bending curling
Trickling splashing
Stopping starting
Adventuring crashing
Growing spreading
One whole link.

Annie Shirt (10)
Suckley Primary School

Down The Hill

Tumbling, tumbling head over heels
Now I know what a roller coaster feels.
Bashing, bashing in the mud
I really hope I don't end up with a thud.
Swishing, swishing in the air
I only just missed a rotten pear.
Jingle, jangle, there goes my money
Ouch, I just hit my tummy.
Rolling, rolling down the dip
Oh no, I look like a tip.
Slowing, slowing, slowing down
I have managed to roll out of town.

Thomas Sandry (11)
Suckley Primary School

The Storm

Lightning, lightning
Frightening, frightening
As fast as lightning
Rain pouring as fast as lightning.

Wayne Scarratt (9)
Suckley Primary School

Rabbit Kennings

Carrot cruncher
Apple muncher
Pink nose
Dinner rose
Soft cheeks
Slight squeaks
Small tail
Feet pale
Green eyes
Little pies
Called Pixie
Is frisky
Black whiskers
Likes pictures.

Georgina Tabberer-Mills (10)
Suckley Primary School

Pony Kennings

Apple cruncher,
Hay muncher.

Jumping gracefully,
Trotting pacefully.

Eyes shimmering,
Coat glimmering.

Tail flashing,
Hooves dashing.

Philippa Jolliffe (10)
Suckley Primary School

Wood Turning

Wood turning fun,
Good, exciting,
Dangerous carver.
Bowls, poles,
Post, host.

Thomas James (10)
Suckley Primary School

Weather Poem

T he thunder rumbles in the distance
H ow loud it seems to be!
U nderestimating its power
N ever has or will be devoured.
D ancing with his friend, Lightning
E nding with them fighting,
R umbling far away
S tarting to get fainter.
T rying to come back
O r retreat to its home,
R oaring with anger
M urdering himself.

Ben Paige (10)
Suckley Primary School

Shogun Total War Kennings

Death bringer
Man slicer
Fierce fighter
Man biter.

James Perrett (8)
Suckley Primary School

Snow Kennings

Winter cold
Frost bold

Ice white
Frost bite

Warm wrap
Frozen tap.

Dannielle Mifflin (9)
Suckley Primary School

Bird Snapper

Rat shaking
Mouse scratching
Bird killer
Bird snapper
Bird heard
Bird quacking.

Joseph Scarratt (7)
Suckley Primary School

Gangster Kennings

Children chaser
Midnight racer
Human killer
Blood filler
Sneaky creepy
Freak peaky
Children screaming
Lights beaming
Cars racing
Police dashing.

Harry Fraser (8)
Suckley Primary School

Shark Kenning

Fish ripper
Blood sipper

Fast swimmer
Catching dinner

Attacks boats
Avoids moats

Big boss
Always cross.

Jamie Bentley (8)
Suckley Primary School

Dolphin

Dolphin splashing in the sea
Making noise in the water looking for its mother
Looking for their mother, jumping over the moon
They are beautiful creatures.

Judy Morris (8)
Suckley Primary School

It's Not The Same Anymore

Its not the same since Scratchy went.
No little head peeping at me through the cage,
No chirping noises,
No warm body wriggling in my arms.

It's not the same anymore.
Rubbish bags lie still and lifeless,
No rustling of exploration.

It's not the same now.
I can't bring myself to call his name,
There's no reason to do so.

His harness hangs on the hook
And his lead is all dusty.

I walk the common with Yanis,
Someone is missing.
No running to keep up with my furry friend.

I can now work and play in peace, uninterrupted,
No inner voice saying, 'It's time to walk Scratchy.'

It's just not the same anymore.
When Scratchy went a small part of me died.

All that's left is an empty cage.
All that's left are the memories -
Hundreds of them . . .

It's just not the same anymore.

Teige Stewart (11)
Wigmore Primary School

Batsmen

B is for boundary surrounding the pitch,
A is for action - catching, batting, bowling.
T is for a ton, a century of runs,
S is for shots, being hit again and again.
M is for maiden over - with no runs scored,
E is for exhausted players after a long, tiring game,
N is for no wins in the season, what an unlucky team!

Kayleigh Luscott (11)
Wigmore Primary School

Cricket Wicket

All the players practising,
Their shirts are all so bright.
Both teams are plotting how they'll win,
They'll both put up a fight.

Wait - what's this?
Movement at last,
The ball is revving,
Speeding fast.

The batsman flicks it in the air,
The ball so shining red,
That wicky fails to cop the ball,
Yet it smacks me on the head!

The bowler obtains the ball once more,
He's racing with a pace.
The batsman's too far in his crease,
Lifts . . .
And wallops me in the face!
Out!

Ben Tranter (11)
Wigmore Primary School

England's Match

Playing cricket is the best,
Wouldn't miss a match, I'm obsessed,
Watching England play a match,
They just caught the winning catch!

England are now starting to bat,
They just hit a six, how about that?
Now all the crowd cry, 'More and more,'
My favourite player has just hit a four.

We're level on points, the crowd starts to roar,
England have just hit the winning four!
Journeying home, singing all the way,
We have had the most brilliant day.

Richard Taylor (10)
Wigmore Primary School

Wild Deer Kennings

Quick creepers,
High leapers,
Bouncy runners,
Love the summers,
Very silent,
Not violent,
Springy walkers,
No talkers.

What am I?

Chloe Reid (10)
Wigmore Primary School

Cricket Poem

He's going to throw me,
He bats, he's going to hit me,
Here I go,
Ow!
The bat hit me!
I'm flying through the air,
Where am I going to land?
It's fun flying in the air,
I'm falling,
Down, down, down,
I'm in the bowler's hand.

Samantha Manuel (10)
Wigmore Primary School

The Cricket Match

It's my innings now, my turn to bat,
I know I won't hit it, I'll probably hear 'Howzat'!
The bowler throws, really fast,
My stomach ties like a knot,
I know this bat will not last.

My shot is a peacher,
The crowd is amazed,
Everyone screams, even my teacher.
I got a whole run, incredible for me,
Nobody knew I would win for my team.

I'm sitting on the bench again,
My bottom goes numb,
People think I'm insane.
The second innings are coming up,
I shall hit the ball alright,
Really thirsty, really thirsty, please give me a cup!

But hold on a minute, people are shouting my name,
'What's going on? What's going on?'
'Someone's out of the game.'
But I'm not ready to play! I stumble onto the pitch,
Wondering what to do,
The ball flies at me like a snitch,
'Howzat!'

Abby Whiteman (10)
Wigmore Primary School

The Ball

Here we go.
I'm ready to be launched
Like a bird in flight.
People cheering,
People screaming.
Ouch! My face is burning red!
Please, please,
Not again!

Sara Crooke (11)
Wigmore Primary School

A Cricket Poem

I strode to the crease,
Bowler is ready to throw,
He grips the ball tight.

Getting squeezed tighter and tighter,
Bowler has thrown the ball,
I swing for the ball.

I have hit their ball,
Ball is hit high in the sky,
I've started running.

The ball has landed,
The ball has rolled over the line,
My score is six more.

The end of the game,
England has won once again,
We're in the final.

Kelly Archer (9)
Wigmore Primary School

We're Batting First

The bowler is waiting patiently,
He bowls the ball,
I hit.
The crowd roar with enthusiasm,
It sails through the air,
Yes, I've got a six.

It's our turn to bowl,
I'm standing still waiting to bowl,
I throw it,
He tries to hit,
But he misses.
It hits the middle stump,
Yes, he's out!

Harry Wright (9)
Wigmore Primary School